Conregational Church of Christ

Manual of the Conregational Church of Christ, North Leominster, Mass.

Conregational Church of Christ

Manual of the Conregational Church of Christ, North Leominster, Mass.

ISBN/EAN: 9783337163655

Printed in Europe, USA, Canada, Australia, Japan

Cover: Foto ©Lupo / pixelio.de

More available books at **www.hansebooks.com**

Manual of the Congregational Church of Christ, North Leominster, Mass. ❧ ❧ ❧

Manual of the Congregational Church of Christ, North Leominster, Mass. ❦ ❦ ❦

J. D. Miller Company, Printers
1898

Contents.

Benevolent Collections

American Missionary Association,	Second Sunday in February.
Church Building Society,	Second Sunday in April.
American Board of Commissioners for Foreign Missions,	
	Second Sunday in June.
Ministerial Aid,	Second Sunday in August.
Home Missions,	Second Sunday in October.
Optional,	Second Sunday in December,
Offering for Church Expenses,	At every Communion service.

History of the Church.

The formation of a Congregational Church in North Leominster was not a matter of sudden thought and action. For several years before any definite step was taken, devout souls in this community were praying for guidance that they might know their opportunity, and be ready to act when God should open the way.

Matters were hastened when it was learned in March, 1874, that the Massachusetts Home Missionary Society was making inquiries about this field. A correspondence was commenced by them. As a result those who felt most earnestly in the matter were called together on the evening of March 24, 1874.

Mr. George S. Burrage was chosen Moderator and Mrs. A. G. Boutelle Clerk. Prayer was offered by Deacon Leonard Wood, after which he presented the following preamble and motion :

" WHEREAS, The Great Head of the Church has been pleased to unite our hearts in an earnest desire for the glory of His name and the salvation of souls ; and

·· WHEREAS, God, by His providential dealings with us, His children, has in the past few weeks plainly spoken to us in a way not to be misunderstood, demanding more and better work for the Master in this neglected part of His vineyard ; and

" WHEREAS, We believe that in order to comply with this demand to the Divine acceptance, it is necessary that a church should be formed in this place, and believing that 'the love of Christ constraining us' has been the grand motive power which has brought us together to consider this subject,

I hereby move that we, members of the Orthodox Congregational Church of Leominster, Mass., do at once take all necessary steps for the forming of a Congregational Church in North Leominster, Mass."

After deliberate consideration this motion was carried.

A committee was chosen to propose Articles of Faith and Covenant ; also one for calling a council to assist in organizing a church.

March 25, 1874, the following letter was sent to the Orthodox Congregational Church of Leominster:

" DEAR BRETHREN AND SISTERS:

WHEREAS, In God's providence we are residents in the village of North Leominster, and feeling that it is our duty to form a Congregational Church in that community, this is to request you to give us such letters of dismission and recommendation as may be suitable in these circumstances."

Then followed the signatures of forty-six members, as given in the chronological list of members. Letters were granted, and upon May 6, 1874, a council of ministers and delegates convened in Kendall Hall, North Leominster, and organized a church known as the Congregational Church of Christ.

The first service after organization was held in Kendall Hall, Sunday, May 17, 1874, Rev. L. H. Sheldon of Andover, Mass., officiating, and continuing to supply the pulpit until November, 1874, when Rev. Henry E. Cooley became pastor.

Church Building.

Soon after the organization of the church, a society was formed under charter granted by the Legislature, and from time to time the subject of building a church was discussed. It seemed to be a great undertaking for the few, and no definite action was taken until March, 1879, when Captain Leonard Burrage presented to the society a lot of land, that a church building might be erected thereon. Steps were immediately taken to raise money for building a church. Ground was broken for the foundation July, 1879, the church was dedicated April 7, 1880, the sermon was preached by Rev. W. J. Batt of Stoneham and the prayer of dedication was offered by the pastor, Rev. E. G. Smith.

For about six years, Sunday services and social gatherings had been held in Kendall hall, the mid-week prayer meeting being held in Union Hall, standing on the lot where the Pierce school building now stands.

The entire cost of the church, including lot and furnishings, was $14,689.71, and there was much delight expressed as Mr. George Hall, Chairman of the Building Committee, read their report, stating that the church was dedicated free of debt.

This church holds in grateful remembrance the names of Captain Leonard Burrage and Mr. Augustus Whitman, who, during their lifetime, gave generously toward the erection and support of the church, and when God called them hence, realizing the need of future years, each left a legacy of five thousand dollars to the society.

Officers of the Church.

PASTORS.

Since this church was organized, twenty-four years ago, seven pastors have served the church, two of whom were installed by councils. Their names, with time of service, are as follows :

Rev. Henry E. Cooley, installed November 10, 1874, died February 17, 1877.

Rev. E. G. Smith, installed June 28, 1877, dismissed July 1, 1881.

Rev. H. P. Cutting, from November 1, 1881, to May 1, 1884.

Rev. N. I. Jones, from March 1, 1885, to March 1, 1887.

Rev. F. A. Balcom, from July 1, 1887, to November 1, 1889.

Rev. H. E. Bray, from January 1, 1890. to July 1, 1893.

Rev. J. M. Bell, from October 1, 1893.

DEACONS.

John H. Shedd, elected June 5, 1874.

Leonard Wood, elected June 5, 1874, resigned September 2, 1880.

Dwight T. Wood, elected September 7, 1880, died December 22, 1892.

Joseph G. Putnam, elected January 20, 1892.

Herbert A. Randall, elected January 18, 1893, resigned January 19, 1897.

Emory F. Burrage, elected January 19, 1897.

CLERKS.

Mrs. Abby G. Boutelle, elected May 6, 1874, retired January 22, 1895.

Mrs. Emma G. Hall, elected January 22, 1895.

TREASURERS.

George Hall, elected May 6, 1874, retired January 25, 1876.

Mrs. S. N. (Fiske) Cowdrey, elected January 25, 1876, retired January 18, 1881.

Lucy E. Shedd, elected January 18, 1886.

Sunday School.

Sunday, May 17, 1874, at the close of the first service held after the organization of the church, a Sunday School was organized, and Deacon Leonard Wood was elected Superintendent, serving the school in this office from May 17, 1874, to April, 1877.

Newton C. Boutelle was then elected, serving until December, 1893.

Herbert A. Randall, elected December, 1893, resigned December, 1895.

Emory F Burrage, elected December, 1895, resigned December, 1898.

Charles H. Haven, elected December 5, 1898.

The school has proved a source of help and strength to the church, a large proportion of the additions to the church having been from the scholars of the Sunday School. For the purpose of a systematic method in the conducting of its work and the transaction of business, the school has adopted the following articles of constitution and by-laws.

. . .

Constitution of Sunday School.

NAME.

ARTICLE 1. This Sunday School shall be known as "The Congregational Sunday School of North Leominster."

OBJECT.

ARTICLE 2. The object of this Sunday School shall be to teach the word of God for the purpose of bringing souls to Christ and of developing Christian character.

MEMBERSHIP.

ARTICLE 3. All persons who shall attend this Sunday School regularly for a period of four weeks may be enrolled as members.

OFFICERS.

ARTICLE 4. The officers of this Sunday School shall be as follows: Superintendent, two Assistant Superintendents, Secretary, Treasurer, Librarian, and an Executive Committee of five, of whom the Pastor, Superintendent and Secretary shall be members. The other two members of the Executive Committee, also the Superintendent and Assistant Superintendent, shall be members of the church.

ANNUAL MEETING.

ARTICLE 5—SECTION 1. The annual meeting shall be held on a week day evening during the first half of December for the election of officers.

SECTION 2. The officers shall be elected by all members of the school, excepting the scholars of the primary department. The Superintendent, Secretary and Treasurer shall be elected by ballot, the other officers may be elected by nomination. Vacancies in office may be supplied at any time by the Executive Committee.

SECTION 3. The school year shall be from January 1 to January 1. Reports shall be read and teachers chosen the first Sunday in January. Teachers may be chosen by the classes subject to the approval of the Executive Committee.

DUTIES OF OFFICERS—SUPERINTENDENT.

ARTICLE 6—SECTION 1. The Superintendent shall conduct the exercises, he shall be Chairman of the Executive Committee, and by all means within his power, both in school and out, shall labor to promote the best interests of the school.

ASSISTANT SUPERINTENDENTS.

SECTION 2. The Assistant Superintendents shall aid the Superintendent as he may need or desire, and supply his place when absent.

SECRETARY.

SECTION 3. The Secretary shall keep a faithful record of all the business transacted by the school and of special gatherings, and shall keep on file all reports of the officers and make a report on the same annually. He shall also keep a weekly record of the attendance and contributions of the school, and report as may be required by the Executive Committee.

TREASURER.

SECTION 4. The Treasurer shall receive and preserve all the funds of the school and pay such bills only as have been approved by two of the Executive Committee; he shall keep a record of all receipts and expenditures, file all bills and vouchers, and make a report to the school at the January meeting

LIBRARIAN.

SECTION 5. The Librarian shall have the care of all the books in the library, and see that they are properly distributed and returned.

EXECUTIVE COMMITTEE.

SECTION 6. The Executive Committee shall select and purchase suitable lesson helps and other literature for the school; they shall appoint the Assistant Librarian, Library Committee and all other committees, and in every way possible they shall provide for the general efficiency and welfare of the school.

DEPARTMENTS.

ARTICLE 7. This Sunday School shall be divided into Primary and Main departments. Bibles and singing books shall be supplied, also graded lesson helps suited to each department.

DUTIES OF TEACHERS.

ARTICLE 8. It shall be the duty of the teachers to prepare themselves well for the lesson, to attend the teachers' meeting, to be punctual and regular at Sunday School, to keep order in the class, to win the affection and hold the attention of the scholars, to present the truth in a practical manner, to pray for, and, if possible, with the scholars; to visit them in their homes, and especially when they are sick, and by legitimate means to try and secure the end for which this school was organized.

SESSIONS.

ARTICLE 9—SECTION 1. This Sunday School shall be held regularly every Sunday, and the exercises shall usually be confined to one hour.

SECTION 2. A special session of the school for the transaction of business may be called at any time by the Superintendent, or upon the request of a majority of the Executive Committee, provided notice of the same has been given at the regular session.

AMENDMENTS.

ARTICLE 10. This constitution may be altered or amended upon recommendation of the Executive Committee at any special session of the school by a two-thirds vote of the members present and voting (see Sec. 2 of Art. 5), provided notice of the proposed amendment has been given at a previous session of the school.

AMENDMENT TO ARTICLE 3—DROPPING MEMBERS.

SECTION 1. Any member of this Sunday School removing from town or attending some other Sunday School in town ceases to be a member. Any member not attending Sunday School may, after a suitable length of time, be dropped by vote of the Executive Committee.

HONORARY MEMBERS.

SECTION 2. All persons who are unable to attend the sessions of the school, yet who still wish to retain their connection with it, may become honorary members. Their names shall be kept in the Secretary's book under the appropriate heading.

. . .

By-Laws.

ARTICLE 1. The Secretary shall make a record of all special addresses given to the school.

ARTICLE 2. It shall be the duty of the Library Committee to select, read and purchase all books for the library.

ARTICLE 3. The newly elected officers shall have power to make all necessary arrangements for the year of service, but the management of the school shall not be turned over to them until the new year.

ARTICLE 4. The Executive Committee shall have power to draw on the Treasurer of the school for necessary lesson helps and literature for the new year.

ARTICLE 5. All collections taken in the school shall be placed in the school treasury, from which shall be paid all bills and appropriations of the school by the Treasurer (in accordance with Sec. 4, Art. 6 of the Constitution). Any class wishing to use their proportional part of the money they have given, above expenses, may do so by applying to the Superintendent for the same, who shall write an order upon the Treasury, stating to whom and for what it is to be paid, signed by two of the Executive Committee.

ARTICLE 6. No business requiring discussion shall come before any regular session of the school.

ARTICLE 7. These by-laws may be altered or amended at any special session of the school by a two-thirds vote of the members present and voting (see Sec. 2 of Art. 5 of the Constitution), provided notice of the same has been given at a previous session.

Young People's Society of Christian Endeavor.

For some time there had been among several of the members of the church a strong feeling that something more was needed for the help of the young people.

In November, 1887, a few of the younger church members were called together by the pastor and Superintendent of the Sunday School to consider the advisability of forming a Christian Endeavor society.

After due deliberation it was decided to form such a society. A meeting was held in the church parlor November 29, 1887, for the purpose of organization.

The meeting was called to order by Mr. N. C. Boutelle. After reciting the 23d Psalm and reading of scripture, prayer was offered by the pastor, Rev. F. A. Balcom. The constitution of the United Society was read and as, sented to by twelve persons as follows: Lucy E. Shedd, Myra L. Merriam Lizzie H. Stone, Carrie L. Wood, Charles Powers, Emma G. Hall, Annie G. Herron, Fannie L. Fiske, Nellie F. Brown, Mattie A. Pierce, Jessie O. Rice, Estella W. Farnsworth.

Officers were elected as follows: President, Carrie L. Wood; Vice-President, Lucy E. Shedd; Secretary, Emma G. Hall; Treasurer, Jessie O. Rice.

The Executive Committee were appointed to make such alterations in the constitution as the needs of our local society seemed to demand.

The society has held its meetings Sunday evenings preceding the regular service, and has been a constant help in all church work.

Junior Society of Christian Endeavor.

The Junior Society of Christian Endeavor was organized January 9, 1897, with a membership of twenty-two. Mrs. J. G. Putnam was chosen Superintendent and Bertha Willard Assistant

Meetings are held for one hour each Friday afternoon, a good interest is manifested and the attendance is very regular. The pastor, Rev. J. M. Bell, who is an active member of the society, gives a talk to the children once in two weeks, which is very helpful. The membership has nearly doubled since the organization of the society.

. . .

Ladies' Benevolent Society.

This society was organized May 21, 1874, the object, as stated in its Constitution, is two fold, " The promotion of social intercourse among ourselves and to aid in the great cause of benevolence at home and abroad." This society aided materially in the building and furnishing of the church, contributing about ($1000) one thousand dollars, and ever since has been ready to lend a helping hand in proportion to the means at its disposal, at the same time keeping up an interest in missions by sending money and clothing to missionaries.

Congregational Principles.

1. THE CHURCH UNIVERSAL.—The visible church universal is composed of those who, believing themselves to be born of the Spirit, publicly confess their faith in Christ as their Saviour and Lord. All Christians, being equally related to the head of the church, are equal in all rights and privileges, and should be in communion with one another.

2. THE SEAT OF CHURCH POWER.—Neither is a single universal church government claiming authority nor one which is national, provincial, diocesan or synodical, warranted by the word of God; but only local congregations (i. e. churches) of believers. These particular churches have all needful power of self-government under Christ, but are to be in recognized communion and cöoperation with each other, including all evangelical churches of whatever name, which will accept such fellowship.

3. THE LOCAL CHURCH.—Those believers who dwell together in one place become a church by their recognition of each other, and their mutual agreement to observe Christ's ordinances in one society.

4. THE FELLOWSHIP OF THE CHURCHES.—But inasmuch as all evangelical churches should be in communion one with another, they should extend to each other the formal recognition of that fellowship, and manifest it by assisting each other with advice and necessary help, by consulting together in all matters of common concern, and by co-operating in work for the advancement of Christ's kingdom.

5. THE CHRISTIAN MINISTRY.—Men who, in the judgment of the churches, are called of God to the ministry of the Word, are by these to be set apart to that service with prayer and laying on of hands. The apostolic injunction, "Lay hands suddenly on no man," requires that due examination be first made as to natural gifts, education, knowledge of the Scriptures, Christian experience and the divine call to preach the Word. Nor is any man to be regarded as retaining fellowship as an ordained minister unless he remain in orderly connection with some body of churches capable of certifying their continued approval.

Confession of Faith and Covenant.

FORM OF ADMISSION.

The candidates shall present themselves before the pulpit, and the minister shall repeat one or more of the following verses of Scripture, or such others as he may choose:

"What shall I render unto the Lord for all His benefits toward me? I will take the cup of salvation and call upon the name of the Lord. I will pay my vows unto the Lord now in the presence of all His people."

"Whosoever, therefore, shall confess Me before men, him will I confess before My Father which is in Heaven."

"For with the heart man believeth unto righteousness; and with the mouth confession is made unto salvation."

The minister shall then address the candidates as follows:

DEARLY BELOVED: You are here. before God and these witnesses, to confess the Lord Jesus Christ and to dedicate yourselves to Him in the everlasting covenant of His grace. Feeling the solemnity and blessedness of this privilege, and praying with us that He who hath begun a good work in you will perform it until the day of Jesus Christ, you now unite with us in this, our common

. . .

Confession of Faith.

1. We believe that there is one God, self-existent, eternal, perfectly holy, the Creator and rightful Disposer of all things, subsisting in a manner mysterious to us, yet revealed in the Scriptures with equal divine attributes as Father, Son and Holy Ghost. Each executing distinct but harmonious offices in the great work of salvation.

2. We believe that the Scriptures of the Old and New Testament were given by the inspiration of God, and contain the only perfect rule of Christian faith and practice.

3. We believe that man, unless renewed by the Holy Spirit, cannot receive salvation.

4. We believe that Jesus Christ, God's only Son, our Lord, took upon Himself our nature, and by tasting death for every man, prepared a way by which all who believe in Him, repenting of their sins, shall receive forgiveness and eternal life; that all such will be kept by the power of God, through faith, in lives of practical obedience unto the end.

5. We believe that for the comfort and strengthening of his followers and in testimony to His truth, our Lord has established in the world a visible church; that it is the duty of all Christians to enter into covenant with it, professing thus their faith in Christ and observing the ordinances of Baptism and the Lord's Supper; that it is the privilege of believing parents to consecrate their children also to God in Baptism, and that all believers, visibly united, though called by different names, are the one body of Christ, severally bound to keep the unity of the spirit in the bond of peace.

6. We believe in the resurrection of the dead, when all will be judged according to the deeds done in the body ; that those who are saved will be saved through their faith in Christ, and those who perish will perish through their unbelief

Thus, so far as you understand, do you believe?

Baptism shall be administered to those candidates who have never been baptized, each kneeling in turn before the table. To those baptized in infancy the pastor will say :

Do you, who in infancy were dedicated to God by your believing parents in the ordinance of Baptism, now declare your personal acceptance of their act and your purpose to continue in the service to which you were then consecrated?

. . .

Covenant.

You do now freely and joyfully enter into the Covenant of Grace. You take the Lord Jesus to be your friend and Saviour, and do declare in entering into the fellowship of this church, that you will, with Divine help, endeavor to honor it in your conversation and life, to do your part towards its temporal support, to labor and pray for its increase, purity and peace, to walk with its members in love and to perform all the duties incumbent upon you as a member of this church.

At this point, those who unite by letter from other churches will rise as their names are called, the pastor saying :

Being already in covenant with God and with His people, you do now,

2

in transferring your peculiar relations to this branch of His church, cheerfully renew the consecration of yourselves to his service.

Do you thus covenant with God and with his people?

Most affectionately, then, do we, the members of this church, receive you to our communion.

This we solemnly attest by rising. With grateful hearts we now own you as our kindred in Christ. We welcome you to all the ordinances and privileges of His church. We break with you this bread of life. We share with you this cup of blessing. We ask your aid in turning to our Master the souls of others. And on our part we covenant with you to offer for you our prayers; to walk with you in sorrow or in joy; seeking advice and strength from you and giving in return the counsel and the aid which you may ask. We promise gladly to render our offices of love, and in all ways, so far as in us lies, to seek your growth in knowledge and in grace, and your perfect meetness for the Heavenly Home.

To Him who is able to keep you from falling and present you faultless before his throne with exceeding joy, we commend the care of your souls. The Lord bless you and keep you. The Lord make his face to shine upon you and be gracious unto you. The Lord lift up the light of his countenance upon you and give you peace. Amen.

Here the pastor, in his own behalf and that of the church, may give to each person the right hand, with such words as the Christian heart, in such circumstances, shall be prompted to utter.

. . .

Rousehold Baptism.

Parents desiring to bring their children for public baptism, are requested to do so, if convenient, on Communion Sabbath, at the opening of the service. They are also requested to give the pastor seasonable notice of their intention, together with the child's name and age.

ADDRESS TO PARENTS.

Jesus said, " Suffer the little children to come unto me, and forbid them not; for of such is the kingdom of God. Verily I say unto you, whosoever shall not receive the kingdom of God as a little child, he shall not enter therein. And he took them up in his arms, put his hands upon them, and blessed them."

BAPTISM.
PRAYER.

Church Discipline.

Offenses against good order in the church are usually spoken of as of two kinds, private and public.

It is the duty of the church to free itself, as far as possible, from complicity with offenses of either kind. Private offenses should be privately removed unless the church is compelled to take public notice of them. If anyone is aware that his brother has aught against him he is to leave everything—the "gift before the altar"—and first be reconciled to his brother. When an offender fails to make reparation the injured one is to go to him and "show him his fault." If harmony is not restored the process of discipline laid down in Matt. xviii: 15-17 is to be pursued. Public offenses require church action from the first. Any member of the church may make charges against the delinquent, or the church may appoint some one to make them. In case of scandalous offenses the church should promptly exclude the guilty one, 1 Cor. v: 3, 5-13; 2 Thess. iii: 6. For some sins evidence of true penitence cannot be given at once. In all cases of discipline the charges of delinquency should be clearly stated in writing. In the church action by which a member is excluded, the reasons for exclusion should be definitely set forth so as at any time to justify this decision.

By-Laws of the Church.

ARTICLE 1. The annual meeting of the church shall be holden in the month of January, at such time and place as the Deacons may appoint, public notice having been given on the previous Sabbath.

ARTICLE 2. The officers of the church shall consist of the Pastor, Deacons, Clerk, Treasurer and Church Committee. The Clerk, Treasurer and Church Committee shall be chosen annually by ballot, and shall serve until their successors are chosen.

ARTICLE 3. The number of Deacons shall be two or more; one shall be chosen for two years and one for three years. After the expiration of these terms they shall be chosen for the term of three years each. They shall aid the pastor in the celebration of the Lord's Supper, shall take charge of the communion service, shall provide for the communion table and shall assist the Pastor generally in the spiritual care of the congregation.

ARTICLE 4. The Clerk shall keep a faithful record of the proceedings of all business meetings of the church, and shall keep a register of the church members, with the date of their reception and of their removal, a record of all baptisms, shall issue letters of dismission voted by the church, keep on file all correspondence, all written official reports and all other valuable papers of the church, and shall make an annual report.

ARTICLE 5. The Treasurer shall have the custody of all the benevolent funds of the church and congregation, disbursing the same under the direction of the Church Committee. His account shall be audited by the Senior Deacon and he shall report at the annual meeting.

ARTICLE 6. The Church Committee shall be the Pastor, the Deacons and four other members of the church, elected annually. They shall examine all persons who may wish to unite with the church, either by letter or profession, and report the same to the church if they shall deem them worthy to become members. They shall determine the time and manner of raising the benevolent contributions of the church and the disposition of the same when not indicated by the donors. They shall have special charge of church discipline and of the transference of membership to and from other churches.

Article 7. At the close of each preparatory lecture a regular church meeting shall be holden for the transaction of business. A special meeting may be called at any time when in the judgment of the Pastor or Deacons it may be deemed expedient, or upon a written request of any five members of the church.

Article 8. The Pastor shall act as Moderator at each church meeting. In case of his absence or of a vacancy in the pastorate, a Moderator *pro tempore* shall be chosen.

Article 9. In case the delegates appointed by the church to attend ecclesiastical bodies should signify their inability to serve, substitutes may be elected by the Deacons.

Article 10. Candidates for admission to the church, on profession of their faith, shall be propounded at least one week previous to their admission.

Article 11. All the members of this church shall enjoy equal religious privileges, and may vote on all questions except those involving finance, discipline and the selection of a pastor. On these latter questions, however, all may vote informally, but in the formal vote only members of twenty-one years of age and over shall be counted.

Article 12. All persons received by this church shall be enrolled as members, but any member residing elsewhere for two years without taking a letter, or any resident member habitually neglecting church ordinances, unless sufficient reason for such neglect appears, may, by vote of the church, be placed upon a " retired list," and such members shall forfeit the right to vote, and for them the church shall cease to be responsible. If, however, any such shall afterward request the rights of full membership, they may be restored by vote of the church.

Article 13. The Sacrament of the Lord's Supper shall be observed on the first Sabbaths of the months of January, March, May, July, September and November. The preparatory lecture shall be given at such time during the week preceding the Communion Sabbath, as may be decided upon by the church.

Article 14. All who love our Lord Jesus Christ and have publicly owned him before men are cordially invited to sit with us at His table.

Article 15. This church regards the making, selling or using of intoxicating drinks as a beverage a violation of covenant obligations.

Article 16. These rules may be altered at any regular church meeting by a vote of a majority of the members present, notice having been given in writing at the last church meeting.

Chronological List of Members.

The letter L. indicates that the person united by letter; D. L. dismissed by letter; R. L. retired list; D. dead; D. W. L. dismissed without letter.

MAY 6, 1874—ORIGINAL MEMBERS.

Allen, Lovisa E.   D. April 30, '85
Burrage, Leonard D.,   D. Apr. 18, '88
Burrage, Myra A.   D. Nov. 10, '81
Burrage, George S.   D. Feb. 25, '77
Burrage. Martha A.
Brown, Mary F.
Boutelle, Newton C.
                        D. L. June 17, '97
Boutelle,Abby G.   D. L. June 17, '97
Cowdrey, Serena (Fiske)
Cleverley, Mary J.
                        D. L. April 30, '78
Derby, George F.   R. L. May, '96
Derby, Catharine R.   R. L. May, '96
Greenleaf, Jennie
                        D. L. March 10, '75
Harris, Anna J. (Wood)
Harris, Annie M.   D. May 7, '75
Hall, George   D. Dec. 15, '94
Hall, Harriet E.
Hartwell, Matilda   D. May 21, '76
Hazard, Nahum G.   R. L. May, '96
Joslin, Luke   D. June 3, '77
Joslin, Elizabeth   D. July 3, '75
Kittredge, Hannah H.
                        D. Aug. 25, '94

Lewis, Laura H. (Wood)
                        D. L. Dec. 30, '81
Lougee, Anna R. (Child)
                        R. L. May, '96
Merriam, Myra L.
Marshall, Rhoda R.   D. Sept. 10, '76
Osborn, Luther
Powers, Charles
Powers, Edly N.   D. July 20, '79
Smith, Lucy J.
Smith, Ella F. (Wood)
Smith, Susan M.   D. Nov. 13, '76
Smith, Alfred M.   D. Aug. 24, '80
Snow, Thomas S.   D. May, '90
Snow, Nancy   D. Jan. 21, '76
Stearns, Sabra E.   R. L. Dec , '98
Shedd, Betsey B.   D. April 18, '79
Shedd, John H.
Shedd, Mary H.   D. Dec. 28, '81
Thompson,Edward P., R. L. May, '96
Thompson, Sarah J.   R. L. May, '91
Wood, Leonard   D. L. Nov. 29, '86
                        D. Feb. 6, 1886
Wood, Julia P.   D. L. Nov. 29, '81
                        L. Aug. 18, '87
                        D. June 25, '91

Wood, Carrie L.   D. L. Dec. 22, '85
     L. Aug. 18, '87
   MAY 6, 1874.
L Johnson, Lydia A., D. July 9, '85
L Wilder, Catherine A.
     D. March 1, '82
   JULY, 1874.
L Osborne, Lucinda, D. Aug, 31, '98
   DECEMBER, 1874.
L Cooley, Rev. Henry E.
     D. Feb. 17, '77
L Cooley, Catharine A.
     D. L. Aug. 31, '77
   JANUARY, 1875.
P Rice, William D. May 11, '95
P Rice, Lucy O. D. April 8, '75
P Willard, Abbie D. L. July, '80
   MAY, 1875.
L Henry, Martha B.
     D. L. Feb. 17, '80
   MAY, 1876.
P York, William D. Jan., '76
L Thurston, Elizabeth A.
     D. Oct. 6, 1880
L Thurston, Judith L.
     D. Oct. 27, '80
   JULY, 1876.
P Kittredge, Myra J.
     D. L. July 8, '79
P Henry, Edwin S.
     D. W. L. May, '91
P Maynard, Mary E. (Field)
     R. L. May, '96
P Rice, Diana
P Shedd, Lucy E.
P Wood, Nellie O. (Stone)
     R. L. May, '96

Wood, T. Dwight D. Dec. 22, '92
Wood, Emeline C.
   JULY, 1877.
P Atherton, Mary P.
     D. Aug. 2,' 77
   DECEMBER, 1877.
L Whitman, Ephraim
     D. L. Dec. 21, '80
L Whitman, Augustina
     D. L. Dec. 21, '80
   JANUARY, 1878.
P Tedford, Samuel R. L. May, '96
L Tedford, Isabella M.
     D. L. April, '95
   MARCH, 1878.
L Parker, Samuel D. L. July, '84
L Parker, Charlotte B.
     D. L. July, '84
   SEPTEMBER, 1878.
L Wood, Abel M. R. L. May, '96
L Wood, Albert R. R. L. May, '96
   NOVEMBER, 1878.
P Tedford, James D. April 18, '85
   JANUARY, 1879.
P Wheeler, Lydia E D. L. Jan., '82
   MAY, 1879.
P Spofford, Frederic S.
     D. Sept. 10, '79
P Spofford, Clara R.
     D. May 22, '79
   MAY, 1880.
L Putney, Charles G.
     D. L. Dec.. '82
L Putney, Izora M. D. L. Dec.. '82
   JULY, 1880.
L Lord, Orlando M., D. L. Dec., '83
L Lord, Isabella D. L. Dec., '83

DECEMBER, 1881.

P Cutting, Rev. Henry P.
  D. L. June, '85

MAY, 1882.

L Burrage, John M. D. Oct. 8, '91
L Burrage, Elizabeth R
  D. Feb. 27, '97

NOVEMBER, 1882.

L Burrage, Nellie G.

MARCH, 1883.

P Stearns, Ellen R. D. Mar. 15, '95

MAY, 1885.

L Rice, Elizabeth D. Nov. 1, '90
L Farnsworth, Estella W.
  D. Jan. 5, '92

L Houghton, Susan E.
  D. July 17, '85

P Burnap, Mary M.

JULY, 1885.

L Herron, Annie G., D. L. May, '89
L Hall, Emma P. G.
L Lear, Alverse D.
L Lear, Delia A.

MARCH, 1886.

L Howe, Carrie E. D. L. Mar., '89

MAY, 1886.

P Powers, Lilla L.

JULY, 1886.

L Putnam, Hannah
P McIntire, George H.
L McIntire, Asenath G.

JANUARY, 1888.

P Stone, Elizabeth H.

MARCH, 1888.

L Balcom, Rev. Frederic A.
  D. L. Oct., '90
L Balcom, Helen E., D. L. Oct., '90

MARCH, 1000.

P Channell, James
L Channell, Sophia S.
P Phelps, Nellie F. (Brown)

MAY, 1889.

P Marden, Jesse K.
  D. L. Oct. 24, '89

JULY, 1889.

L Lord, George W.
  D. Sept. 25, '99

P Smith, Addie E. (Derby)

SEPTEMBER, 1890.

L Dodge, Lucina E.

MAY, 1890.

P Alger, Addie C., D. L. June 29, '91
L Bray, Rev. Henry E.
  D. L. Oct. 25, '94
L Bray, Sarah M., D. L. Oct. 25, '94
L Hartwell, Eliza A.
L Preston, Ada L. B.
  D. W. L. Sept., '94

SEPTEMBER, 1890.

P Shedd, Mary C.

JANUARY, 1891.

L Putnam, Joseph G.
L Putnam, Anna G.
L George, Mary L. D. Aug. 14, '93
P Porter, Grace R. (Pierce)
P Hatch, Lucie M. D. L. April, '93
L Rice, Jessie O.
L Randall Herbert A.
L Randall, Anna E.

MARCH, 1891.

P Armstrong, Sarah M.

MAY, 1891.

P Fiske, Frank N.
P Fiske, Fannie L.

NOVEMBER, 1891.
P   Burrage, Emory F.
L   Kendall, Rhoda A.
L   Kendall, Flora E.
        JANUARY, 1892.
L   Lewis, Sabra
L   Lewis, Mary A.
L   Parkhurst, Arthur H.
P   Parkhurst, Nora L.
        NOVEMBER, 1892.
L   Jewett, Charles A., D. L. Dec., '94
L   Jewett. Pearl A.   D. L. Dec., '94
        NOVEMBER, 1893.
L   Bell, James M.
L   Bell, Susan F.
        NOVEMBER, 1894.
L   Haven, Charles H.
L   Haven, Helen A.
        JULY, 1896.
P   Baker, Eva A.
P   Burchstead, Walter H.

L   Bell, Enoch F.
P   Burrage, Leonard J,
                D. Oct. 26, '98
P   Newell, Della Conant
P   Walker, Alice M.
        NOVEMBER, 1896.
L   Whitney, Catharine L.
        JANUARY, 1897.
L   Putnam, Artemas
L   Putnam, Mary O.
P   Baker, Elmer W.
        MARCH, 1897.
L   Burchstead, Luthera A.
P   Bell. Sidney E.
P   Brown, Ida
L   Pierce, Mattie E.
L   Walker, Jennie
        MAY, 1897.
P   Burrage, Royden F.
P   Burrage, Marion G.

Alphabetical List of Present Members.

Avery, Sarah M. (Armstrong)
Burrage, Martha A.
Burrage, Emory F.
Burrage, Nellie G.
Burrage, Royden F.
Burrage, Marion G.
Brown, Mary F.
Brown, Ida
Burnap, Mary M.
Bell, Rev. James M.
Bell, Susan F.
Bell, Enoch F.
Bell, Sidney E.
Burchstead, Luthera A.
Burchstead, Walter H.
Baker, Elmer W.
Baker, Eva A.
Cowdrey, Serena N.
Channell, Sophia S.
Channell, James P.
Dodge, Lucina E.
Fiske, Frank N.
Fiske, Fannie L.
Harris, Anna J.
Hall, Harriet C.
Hall, Emma P. G.
Hartwell, Eliza A.
Haven, Charles H.
Haven, Helen A.

Lewis, Mary L.
McIntire, George H.
McIntire, Asenath G.
Merriam, Myra L.
Newell, Della M.
Osborne, Luther
Powers, Charles
Powers, Lilla L.
Putnam, Hannah
Putnam, Joseph G.
Putnam, Anna G.
Putnam, Artemas
Putnam, Mary O.
Porter, Grace R.
Phelps, Nellie G.
Parkhurst, Arthur H.
Parkhurst, Nora L.
Pierce, Mattie A.
Rice, Diana
Rice, Jessie O.
Randall, Herbert A.
Randall, Anna E.
Smith, Ella F.
Smith, Lucy J.
Smith, Addie E.
Shedd, John H.
Shedd, Lucy E.
Shedd, Mary C.
Stone, Elizabeth H.

Kendall, Flora E.
Kendall, Rhoda A.
Lear, Alverse D.
Lear, Delia A.
Lewis, Sabra

Walker, Jennie
Walker, Alice M.
Whitney, Catharine L.
Wood, Carrie L.
Wood, Emeline C.